GOD
SAID IT!

A Historical Review of the Voice of
God and Humanity's Future

BRUCE E. VORAN

Copyright © 2022 Bruce E. Voran
All rights reserved
First Edition

Fulton Books
Meadville, PA

Published by Fulton Books 2022

ISBN 979-8-88505-405-8 (paperback)
ISBN 979-8-88505-406-5 (digital)

Printed in the United States of America

INTRODUCTION

In *God Said It!* there are certain assumptions which are taken with regard to the voice of God that everyone may not understand or subscribe to on the same level. History does have its own sympathetic followers who may, but not necessarily, attempt to find themselves within history. In reality, the projection by anyone into a historical perspective is presumptive. The projection itself is theoretical at best having not been a first-hand witness to or a participant in those historical events. Current historical events are the exception in that one exists and in existence makes personal interpretations, understandings, acceptance, and projections possible. Such may be entirely different for other contemporary witnesses.

God Said It! makes no pretense of being a compendium of historical knowledge from prehistory to the present. It does attempt to draw a line from prehistory to the present. The line is drawn and runs through historical events generally known by many. Running under that line is a stream of consciousness that God or gods may exist and are understood as God or gods by those living in the historical events, myths, or realities. The line also tends to confirm the maxim that history tends to repeat itself. A singular personal understanding of the past is presented and makes a projection of that understanding into a contemporary perspective. It is not intended to be pedagogical or narrow in its presentation to the exclusion of other assumptions, understandings, or perspectives. It is a personal assumptive statement that allows for a concurrent acceptance in whole or part or for its complete or partial dismissal. Or why else does *God Said It!* end with as statement recorded in Joshua 24:15?

References to the Old (First) Testament, New (Second) Testament, and general references to the Quran will be mentioned. Much will rely without annotations on anthropologic, historic, theological, and genealogical research as interpreted by various authors.

Where it was reasonably possible when prehistory or recorded history events are mentioned, a presumption is made to be involved within those reported events and wonder what one would be doing and observing at the time. Such presumptive observations can only be the result of conjecture. It would be impossible to totally disassociate oneself from one's own history, perceptions, and reality and then be a participant in an event that occurred in a different time frame. The accuracy of those presumptions cannot be considered absolute. The door is open, however, should anyone choose any interpretation of the referenced events as used in *God Said It!* The same must be said regarding the line of thought that reaches from prehistory into the present and potentially future events. References, presumptions, and interpretations must remain personal. Absolute truth can only be presumed to be true.

CHAPTER 1

Presumptive Beginnings

It may be assumed that prehistory hominids could have had a cognitive capacity to discern whether an event in their natural world was reasonable or of unknown origin. A sudden flood, a lightning strike, the disappearance of certain necessary food sources, and encounters with invasive other hominids are only a few unexplained phenomena that might have given rise to some primitive and speculative thoughts. These thoughts could be the precursors of beliefs in power sources beyond the hominid's natural world. Presumably, explanations of such power sources can give rise to mysticism, mythology, and all sorts of necessary sacrifices. Cannibalism, human sacrifices, offerings to the unknown power source, dances, songs, and totems could be considered precursor activities directed at that which recorded history eventually call gods. In the period before recorded history for the prehistoric hominid, and therefore undocumented, the unknown power sources might be considered a God or gods who spoke to the hominid, a human creature.

Necessary for a complete understanding of the voice of God and of that developed in primeval history is first to trace the origins of the species known as man. The species to which modern man belongs originated in Africa as *Homo sapiens* arising from an earlier species and more ape-like *Homo erectus* that first appeared about two million years ago. Europe, China, and Indonesia are locations where *Homo erectus* fossils have been found. There is a school of thought that *Homo sapiens* emerged from Africa approximately one hundred thousand years ago and replaced earlier species. *Homo heidelbergensis* also migrated out of Africa as did *Homo neanderthalensis* with whom *Homo sapiens* may have mated throughout their range. From the British Isles, north through China and across a land bridge to North America, along the coast line to Southeast Asia, and through the Pacific Islands to Central America, various species' DNA are found. Some stayed close to Africa in an area called the Levant, between the Tigris and Euphrates rivers, and that can be called Ancient Israel. It's about them the First (Old) Testament of the Bible came to be a record.

By 12,000 BCE during the Neolithic Period, peoples, and hunter-gathers were in Mesopotamia or the *land between the rivers*. Permanent dwellings and other signs of modern civilization were developed here. The area between the Tigris and Euphrates rivers was called the Fertile Crescent. Its borders are modern-day Iraq, Syria, Turkey, and Iran. Regular flooding made the land fertile and ideal for growing crops. Complex societies developed that included writing, architecture, governments, division of labor, and societal classes, all of which are called characteristics of civilization. Around 3400 BCE (the Bronze Age as an approximate period), the Fertile Crescent would see the rise of Zoroastrianism and ultimately Judaism. And while it is likely that humans worshipped gods before then, it was before the Iron Age (1200–600 BCE as an approximate period) that evidence was seen for organized monotheistic religion. Strict monotheism emerged.

Earlier Hebrew henotheism which worshipped God but didn't deny other gods became the exclusive worship of the God of Israel (YHWH) as prescribed in the Torah and practiced at the Temple of Jerusalem.

CHAPTER 2

Early Beginnings of Recorded History

The Old (First) Testament is in the form of a historical narrative. The Pentateuch, the first five books of the Old (First) Testament, or the Torah are sometimes called *the book of Moses*. However, as of the late nineteenth century, assigning Moses as the author has been called into question. Many biblical scholars believe that these written books were begun to be written and finally revised between the sixth-century BCE and the fifth-century BCE. These books likely were based on earlier written sources and existing oral traditions. Verifying dates or history of events in the Pentateuch is difficult. Dating history beginning with the period of the Judges becomes more reliable. The first books include the Creation stories, ancient ancestors, Exodus, and the conquest of Canaan under Moses and Joshua.

The order of the Old (First) Testament is the following: (1) the Torah or Law, the five books of the Pentateuch (Genesis, Exodus, Leviticus, Numbers, and Deuteronomy); (2) the Prophets, consisting of Joshua, Judges, First and Second Samuel, First and Second Kings, Isaiah, Jeremiah, Ezekiel, and the Twelve (or Minor) Prophets; (3) the Writings. Together, these represent sixty-six books. Some editions of the First (Old) Testament include seven additional books called the Apocrypha; Tobit, Judith, Wisdom of Solomon, Sirach (also called Ecclesiasticus), Baruch, First and Second Maccabees. These are often considered doubtful authenticity but are often widely circulated as true. Apocrypha, meaning *the hidden things* are the biblical books received by the early Church as part of the Greek version of the Old (First) Testament but not included in the Hebrew Bible being excluded by the non-Hellenistic Jews from their canon. These books are considered as not divinely inspired but are worthy of study by the faithful.

That told in the Book of Genesis arose during a period of mysticism and mythology in which is found the story of Noah and his descendants. The reliability of the story of Noah and his descendants from a contemporary perspective is on the same level as assigning truth to the storyline of the movie *The Da Vinci Code* or Agatha Christie's novel *Murder on the Orient Express*. Reliable or not, the story of Noah and his descendants is reasonably held by those of faith as something of value and of that which allegedly follows. The story of the Genesis flood narrative (Genesis 6–9) is a theme of God's anger provoked by sin and, therefore, divine retribution. Noah was seen as righteous in a world full of iniquity. Genealogically, Noah was the son of Lamech and the ninth in descent from Adam. Terah, the ninth descent from Noah, was the father of Abram, Nahor, and Haran.

For the purposes of which is to follow, a message in whatever form taken from God will be referred to as a "Pentecostal event."

To understand the voice of God throughout the Bible and the Quran, a review of Pentecostal events in a larger context must reference the Noahic flood narrative. Noah's flood is one of the most ancient, but not the oldest, religious stories in the world. Older than the Noah story is the flood mentioned in the Babylonian Epic of Gilgamesh. The Epic of Gilgamesh is assumed by some researchers to be the basis for the Noahic narrative. The five Sumerian poems about Bilgamesh (Sumerian for Gilgamesh), who was the king of Uruk, date from the Third Dynasty (2100 BCE) of Ur. Regarded as one of the earliest surviving notable pieces of literature, this epic poem from ancient Mesopotamia is the second oldest religious text after the *Pyramid Texts*. The older *Pyramid Texts* (2613–2181 BCE) contain mortuary prayers, hymns, and spells from Egypt intended to protect a dead king or queen and ensure life and sustenance in the hereafter.

Assumed to be built on the Epic of Gilgamesh, the Genesis flood narrative is a theme of lack of faithfulness to God, except for Noah, and would result in penalties. God speaks to Noah (a Pentecostal event), and here is possibly the first covenant, the Noahic Covenant, between God and man. This type of covenant is similar to a legal agreement. Promises are agreed to by all parties. Faithfulness is rewarded, and lack of faithfulness is punished. The flood narrative and the Noahic Covenant foreshadow the Abrahamic Covenant arising in the Sodom and Gomorrah story. The Abrahamic Covenant is a promissory agreement and was a central concern in later Judaism. This agreement with the Creator established the status of the Jews as the chosen people and the promising of a future leader or king from the Davidic line. The *promise* obligated both parties to be faithful or else the agreement would be broken.

Within the Judeo-Christian and Islamic traditions, this story, the flood narrative, is told and retold. A flood is also told and retold in Chinese, Polynesian, Hindu, Norse, Native American, South American, New Zealand, and Australian (to mention a few) mythologies. The ending of the last glacial period and the sudden rise in sea levels could have inspired various tales. Many often tend to emphasize the floods as a period of cleansing or retribution directed by some form of deity and the rebirth of humanity.

In virtually all flood narratives, there is a *hero* who seeks to gain or recover life in a better form. The floods in Genesis and in Surah 11 and Surah 71 of the Quran are often referred to as fable-like or legendary and prefatory to characters and events which are told later. The story of Moses and the Exodus from Egypt, which is related as occurring around 1450 BCE, and the giving of the Law, the Pentateuch, and conquest of Canaan can be about the characters, events, cleansing, and retribution that follow the flood story. And, too, the Sodom and Gomorrah narrative can be seen as an extension of the theme related to the flood narrative.

CHAPTER 3

Recorded History Continued

In recorded history, it is believed God has spoken many times and in significant ways and is heard deep in history as recorded in the Old (First) and New (Second) Testaments of the Bible and later in the Quran. Jesus promised that the Holy Spirit would be a Helper for His people.

> But the Helper, the Holy Spirit, whom the Father will send in My name, He will teach you all things, and bring to your remembrance all that I said to you. (John 14:26 NIV)

In liturgically inclined Christian denominations, the Feast of Pentecost is a festival which marks the descent of the Holy Spirit on the disciples as recorded in Acts 2. Pentecost comes from the Greek word for fiftieth. For Christians, Pentecost is a festival that occurs seven Sundays after Easter (Easter plus forty-nine days equaling fifty days.) For Jews, there are *Pentecostal* festivals except they didn't call them Pentecostal. A reference to Hebrew feasts is recorded in Exodus 23 and 24, Leviticus 16, Numbers 28, and Deuteronomy 16. The Hebrew word for *weeks* is *Shavuot*. Pentecost is the Greek name for Shavuot and literally means *fiftieth day*. The Feast of Weeks occurs fifty days or seven weeks after Passover. Christians observe the Feast of Pentecost seven weeks after Easter.

Shavuot is a celebration of harvest for the Jews. There were two harvests every year. The first is in early spring and the second comes in the fall. There were various observations of which one was of unleavened bread and the Feast of Firstfruits. Passover and that of unleavened bread are basically considered the same. Passover was an event in which the people of Israel were freed from their bondage in Egypt. It was a time when Jews were given the Torah and became a nation committed to serving God. The Feast of Firstfruits took place during the week-long Passover celebration as recorded in Leviticus 23:4–8.

> The Lord said to Moses, "Speak to the Israelites and say to them: 'When you enter the land I am going to give you and you reap its harvest, bring to the priest a sheaf of the first grain you harvest.'" (Leviticus 23:9 NIV)

Beginning with Firstfruits and counting fifty days is the beginning of the wheat harvest. Because it always was seven weeks, this event is called the Feast of Harvest or the Feast of Weeks. Acts 2 records that the disciples gathered together for the Feast of Harvest when their room was filled with the Holy Spirit-a notable Pentecostal event. The Feast of Weeks/Harvest was a time for Jews to make a pilgrimage to the Temple in Jerusalem in which all men would bring their first fruits as an offering or sacrifice to God.

The Book of Deuteronomy reads that the First/Solomon's Temple was built in 957 BCE and was a place of offering or sacrifice. It replaced the Tabernacle built under the direction of Moses. The Babylonians in 586 BCE destroyed the First Temple. In 516 BCE, the Second Temple was built only to be destroyed by the Romans in 70 CE. The building of a Third Temple has never been realized.

Historical records reveal that the armies of Rome overcame/captured Jerusalem in 63 BCE. Rome allowed various Hebrew religious practices to continue. Mary and Joseph travel to Bethlehem on Roman orders to be taxed. Forty days after the birth of Jesus, Mary presented herself at the Temple in Jerusalem to satisfy the purification requirements in Leviticus 12. They also go to present Jesus before God and make an offering of two young birds (Luke 2:22–35).

Monotheistic and polytheistic religious views created fictions. The First Jewish Revolt in 66 CE was the result of oppressive taxation and variously held religious views. A Jewish group called the Sicarii took over the Masada complex overlooking the Dead Sea. Around the time of the Passover in 70 CE, the Romans allowed the pilgrims entry into Jerusalem to worship at the Second Temple. The Romans then encircled Jerusalem trapping the pilgrims inside, withdrawing food and water that eventually led to their starvation. The Romans also destroyed the Second Temple. All that remained was the West Wall which is a site of prayer and pilgrimage today.

The fighting did not end in 70 CE. The Sicarii held out at Masada until 73 CE. When it became clear the Romans were about to overtake Masada, nearly all the Sicarii took their lives. Rather than becoming Roman slaves, mass suicide was preferred. Only two women and five children who hid in the cisterns survived to tell the story of Masada.

As a result of the Second Temple's destruction in 70 CE, the Feast of Weeks/Harvest moved from an agricultural feast to a commemoration of the giving of the Law (the Torah) on Mount Sinai. The Feast of Weeks/Harvest (Shavuot) becomes a synagogue celebration where there is a reading of the Torah, meals of dairy foods, and an all-night study of the Book of Ruth.

For Christians, Jews, and Muslims, any Pentecostal event is a time to celebrate God speaking to His created both individually and collectively. This speaking of God to His created almost always is a voice heard from which there is no known physical source. A prime example is the voice of God coming from a burning bush as experienced by Moses. The inspiration of the Holy Spirit to Simeon as recorded in Luke 2:25–26 is a variation of the *no known physical source* reference. The sound of rushing wind and the tongues of fire on the day of Pentecost for the Disciples in Acts 2:1–5 is another example. An exception to *no known physical source* is the Archangel Gabriel speaking to both Mary who was to give birth to Jesus and

Muhammed who was instructed to recite/write the Quran. For most, however, the voice of God is often perceived as an *aha* event.

An *aha* is seen as a moment of inspiration, comprehension, insight, or recognition. For those who accept the concept of a God speaking to His creation, the *aha* event can qualify in that there is no visible presence speaking but a message is perceived. However, caution must be taken with the perception identified as an *aha* event. Some *aha* events can simply be the choice to use one tool over another, to take a different route to work or which different herb to put into a soup dish for supper. A discerning process must be used to distinguish between an intuitive generated action and an action generated as the result of a recognition that the voice of God is heard. Even a meditative generated response can be in error as the human hearer is still a fallible creation. Fallible or true, the perception of the message, whether for good or evil, can lead to dramatic action and meaning such as the good recorded as that just mentioned in Acts 2 wherein there was a rushing of wind and the disciples suddenly were able to communicate in languages that before they were unable to do.

CHAPTER 4

Sodom and Gomorrah Explored

Three riders approach the home of Abram and Sara who invite the riders to eat. Two of the riders are on their way to destroy Sodom and Gomorrah in which Abram's nephew Lot lives. Abram asks the riders, "What if you find fifty righteous in Sodom? Or how about forty-five or forty? Or…" The count goes down to ten. The biblical stories in Genesis 18 and 19 concerning Sodom and Gomorrah are interpreted variously. At root, the two legendary cities were destroyed by God for their wickedness. The wickedness has variously been interpreted as inhospitality, failure to care for those less fortunate, and, most prominently, sexual lust and homosexuality. The refusal to care for the poor despite the prosperity of the inhabitants is mentioned in Ezekiel 16:49. This is taken as further evidence that homosexuality is not the sole cause of their damnation. The Quran, also, contains a version of the two cities in which the evil in Sodom and Gomorrah is a reference to *indecency* and is followed by a reference to highway robbery and other *evil deeds*.

The outrage at Gibeah as told in Judges 19–20 parallels the story of Sodom and Gomorrah in Genesis 18–19. Outsiders or travelers were given shelter and hospitality by a native resident in both stories. The hospitable household is attacked by the male towns folk demanding sexual access to the travelers. In Sodom and Gomorrah, the travelers are angels who use their power to save the household and bring an end to the violence. The cities are then destroyed. In Gibeah, a Levite, an Israelite, and his concubine are given shelter by a Benjaminite, an Israelite. The Benjaminite casts, in place of the Levite from Ephraim, the Levite's concubine to a mob who then pack rape her to death. In Gibeah, all the protagonists are Israelites, and there is no divine intervention.

The story concludes with a genocidal civil war among the Israelites. With Gibeah, because a woman is raped to death, the story has played no part in homophobic ideology. Nonetheless, the Gibeah story clearly demonstrates that the event related to Judges is a tale of attempted rape and humiliation of a male outsider and so should not be read as a tale of same-sex love and desire. In Genesis 18–19, rape is also a hostile act intended to humiliate, debase, if not murder, the two angelic riders.

A seldom emphasized aspect of both the Sodom and Gomorrah and Gibeah stories is twofold, or possibly threefold. First, the rape of a male by other males takes the *honor* away from the raped male who then is *feminized*. As such, he is seen to have the value of a woman. Second, the value of a female was worth no more than simple property. This was demonstrated in both the Genesis and Judges stories. Lot, in place of the two riders, offers to the angry male town folks his virgin daughters. And in doing so, he intends to save the *honor* of the two riders who were guests in his house. In Gibeah, the Benjaminite host, who has total control of whom or whatever is in his house, gives the Levite's concubine to the angry males who gang rape her to death. By extension, the Levite's *honor* is compromised because it was his concubine, his property, that was raped. He takes the body of his concubine back to Ephraim, cuts her into twelve pieces, and demonstrates to the Israelites in Ephraim the injustice and the attack on his *honor*. This is how the Israelite genocidal civil war is started.

Seeking vengeance for what happened in Gibeah, the other tribes of Israel (except for the tribe of Machir) begin a genocidal civil war as recounted in the Book of Judges against the tribe of the youngest son of Jacob and Rachel. Almost all of the members of Benjamin were wiped out by other Israelite tribes, including women and children. Only six hundred Benjamin men survived. However, none of the other Israelite tribes would be willing to give their daughters in marriage to the men of Benjamin. To circumvent this, the men of the tribe of Machir were killed because they showed no concern for the almost lost tribe of Benjamin. Four hundred virgin women from the tribe of Machir were given in marriage to the Benjamin surviving men. This still left two hundred who were without wives. At an upcoming Israelite festival where women came to dance, these two hundred hid in the vineyards and *grabbed* a wife each, took them back to their land, and built houses (Judges 19–21).

Perhaps as a possible third view, it can be argued that a lesser view or value of females as one of the two sexes as accounted in the Sodom and Gomorrah and Gibeah stories reaches back to the Adam and Eve narrative. Interpretations and beliefs regarding Adam and Eve and the serpent and the story revolving around them vary across religions and sects. Both Adam and Eve were responsible for their sins of disobedience, but they repented, asked for forgiveness and God forgave them in the Islamic version of the story. It needs to be noted that in the Quran, only Mary, the mother of Jesus, is mentioned and Eve is never mentioned by name as Eve except by inference as Adam's spouse. Adam's spouse is seen only as an accomplice to human sin and not the instigator.

The Quranic story of Adam and Eve differs from Jewish and Christian traditions. In the Jewish and Christian traditions, Adam and Eve do suffer the consequences of their disobedience by living mortal lives on earth. The consequences were a lifetime of hard labor and death for the man and pain of childbirth and subordination to her husband for the woman. The serpent is to go on his belly and suffer the hatred of both man and woman.

This is the curse for all three from God. In many contemporary Middle Eastern Islamic countries, females are still considered of less value and subordinate to males. However, there is a rise in Islamic feminism in many Middle Eastern countries. Until the twentieth century in many Western societies, the place of females was secondary to males and have roots that also reach very deep. Still equality in Western and Eastern countries has yet to be realized where equality as a value is completely realized between females and males. The same can be said of the inequality between racial, ethnic, religious, and cultural groups where equality has yet to be realized.

The *sins* of Sodom and Gomorrah have been variously interpreted as inequity, adultery, pridefulness, cruelty, lack of hospitality, extortion, oppressing the poor and the needy, and often, homosexuality. With regard to homosexuality, the terms *sodomy* and/or *sodomite* do not arise until the Middle Ages. At least from the Middle Ages in Christianity, Sodom and Gomorrah have long represented the evils of same-sex love and desire. In contrast, however, Rabbinic Judaism understood Sodom and Gomorrah as archetypes for injustice, cruelty, and hatred of outsiders. Sodom and Gomorrah as the archetype of inhospitality to outsiders is found in the Gospel According to Luke (Luke 17:20–37). Jesus warns in the Gospel of Matthew of a worse judgment for some cities than Sodom and Gomorrah. The sin is of inhospitality or of being impenitent.

> If anyone will not welcome you or listen to your words, leave that home or town and shake the dust off your feet. Truly I tell you, it will be more bearable for Sodom and Gomorrah on the day of judgment than for that town. (Matthew 10:14–15 NIV)

The modern idea of sexual orientation didn't always exist in biblical times. The powerful love story of Jonathan and David in 1 and 2 Samuel suggests that the love between same-sex couples is affirmed and blessed by God. It's impossible to know whether David and Jonathan expressed their love sexually. There are various translations which express the great love between Jonathan and David.

> I grieve for you, Jonathan my brother; you were very dear to me. Your love for me was wonderful, more wonderful than that of women. (Samuel 1:26 NIV)

In contemporary terms, David may have been bisexual in that he committed adultery with Bathsheba and later made her one of his eight wives and also considered Jonathan as *more wonderful than that of women*. The foreshadowing of the genealogical importance of David in the lineage of Mary and thus to Jesus is mentioned in 1 and 2 Samuel. The gospels of Matthew and Luke give two different accounts that trace Jesus through Mary back to David. It is through David that the genealogy of Jesus is traced in Matthew (1:1–26) and Luke (1:32–33 and 3:23–28) that he is the legitimate Hebrew Messiah. Before David and Mary, the mother of Jesus, however, must come the narrative of Abraham, Sarah, and their sons, Isaac and Ismael.

CHAPTER 5

First Covenant Developed and the Importance of Isaac and Ismael

The meeting of the three riders and Abram begins a covenant built on a legal agreement, a Promissory Covenant, which included penalties and rewards. This *legal* agreement mirrors the flood narrative and the Sodom and Gomorrah narrative in that God punishes those who were unfaithful. It can also be understood that God punishes the powerful who abuse their power thereby causing suffering for those less powerful. Abram and his nephew Lot were rewarded under this *legal* agreement for their faithfulness. God, seen as one of the three riders who came visiting, declared Abram's new name *Abraham*. He would be a father of many nations and promised land and descendants as numerous as the stars as a reward for his faithfulness. This is the Abrahamic Covenant which lasts until today.

One of the three riders said they would return in a year after having taken care of Sodom and Gomorrah and stated that Sarah will bear a son in a year. Both Abraham and Sarah have a good laugh. Abraham about one hundred and Sarah around ninety-one were childless. There was no son. Abraham won't have descendants as numerous as the stars. So Sarah turns over to Abraham's bed her handmaiden, Hagar, a servant girl from Egypt. Hagar produces a boy named Ishmael. Sarah does have a son within the year, and the child is named Isaac.

Ishmael, from whom arises the Arab Ishmaelites, and Hagar had to be sent away to Egypt so that Isaac would be Abraham's only and true heir. The story begins to deepen as this rejection of Ishmael will become the tradition called Islam.

Several Arab tribes are considered the descendants of Ismael's twelve sons. The number 12 plays a large role in both the Old (First) Testament and the New (Second) Testament. Ismael has twelve sons. Isaac has twelve sons. Jacob has twelve sons. Twelve unleavened cakes of bread are to be presented in the temple every week. There are twelve disciples. There are twelve Minor Prophets. The number twelve was considered to be a perfect number. Muhammad, a descendant of one of Ismael's twelve sons, was born in 570 CE. Muhammad, at the age of 40, is believed to have received revelations, a Pentecostal event, that would become the Quran in a cave called Hira, located on the mountain Jabal an-Nour, near Mecca. The Archangel Gabriel is said to have instructed Mohammad to recite/write what was to become the Quran, the holy book of Islam. These revelations continued to the end of his life in 632 CE. He did not name a successor.

Two major factions of the several Arab tribes emerge at this point. The Shi'a believed only a direct ancestor of Muhammad could guide the Muslim community. The closest blood relative of Muhammad would be their next leader or caliph. The Sunni faction thought the next leader should be determined by consensus and elected three from Muhammad's most trusted companions. Whether the succession of Muslim leadership or caliphs and the succession of leadership in the developing Christian community is an intertwining history may be questionable.

However, a Christian hierarchy seems to have developed by the late first century and early-second century based on a belief that Jesus granted Peter jurisdiction (Matthew 16:18–19) over the developing Church. The successors of Peter would eventually be elected and called popes. Relative to caliphs, the Islamic community remains divided today. The Sunni are in the majority and occupy most of the Muslim world. The Shi'a populations are concentrated in Iran and Iraq as well as Bahrain, Lebanon, Kuwait, Turkey, Pakistan, and Afghanistan.

Other stories of similar natures follow the theme of faithfulness and rewards and are recorded in the Old (First) Testament and the Quran. God tells Abraham to take Isaac up the hill and sacrifice him. God stops faithful Abraham and offers a ram in Isaac's place. The same story is in the Quran except God tasks Abraham to sacrifice Ishmael. God stops Abraham here, too, as a reward for Abraham's steadfast allegiance to God. In one case, the reward is a ram and in the other a great national alliance or Islam.

The Promissory Covenant is in full display in these two stories. Full devotion to God is rewarded. Less than full devotion would result in punishment resulting in the death of a firstborn. The firstborn must survive and reproduce in order for the chosen people to continue throughout history. In the Jewish tradition, Isaac is spared and takes as his wife Rebecca. Ishmael, who is to be the father of a great nation, has twelve sons, mighty princes (Genesis 17:20), and one daughter, Mahalath, who becomes the third wife of Esau, the son of Isaac and Rebecca. Ishmael's mother Hagar, is, according to Rabbinic sources, thought to be Pharaoh's daughter who arranges the marriage of Ishmael to the daughter of Pharaoh and, therefore, Ishmael's sons would be princes.

The intertwining of Israelite and Arab stories is reasonable in that each culture or people tended to occupy adjacent lands and had interchanging economic and/or personal relations. The Israelite stories that appear in the Old (First) Testament were codified five or six centuries before Mohammad was directed in a Pentecostal event by the Archangel Gabriel to recite/write what was to become the Quran. It is unreasonable to assume that the older Israeli writings, as well as that written before the beginning of the second century of the Christian Era as recorded in the New (Second) Testament, were not known in the Arab communities and did not have a role or influence in the Quran's development.

Setting this speculation aside, there is an inference in the telling about Ishmael and Isaac that Ishmael would attempt to overtake and take the place of Isaac as the true *firstborn* of Abraham. The conflict between Isaac and Ishmael could explain the animosity that developed between Israeli and Arab cultures. Both Isaac and Ishmael apparently attended the funeral of Abraham. It is at Abraham's funeral (Genesis 25:9) that Isaac found he has inherited all of his father's property, and this may have been an injurious insult to Ishmael. Yet the two bury their father as brothers. However, the animosity between Isaac and Ishmael about who was born first would foreshadow the saga of Isaac's two sons, Jacob and Esau.

CHAPTER 6

Moses

The continuing story of Isaac and his wife Rebecca leads to the relationship between their fraternal twins, Jacob and Esau. The son named Jacob, also called Israel, was to be the father of the twelve tribes. A conflict arises between their descendant nations as a result of Jacob's deception of their old blind father Isaac. Esau loses his birthright. Having been born first before Jacob, Esau should have had the birthright (Genesis 25). Of the two nations that develop, the nation of Esau would forever be the lesser of the two. The elder of the two nations would be less than the younger nation.

Esau would have only five sons but apparently did have twelve grandchildren. The Edomites are the descendants of Esau. Edomites and Israelites, those descendants from Jacob, were constant enemies. The Edomites tried to conquer the country of Israel during the time of Jehoshaphat but didn't succeed. Both Saul and later David defeated the nation of Edom. The Edomites allied with Nebuchadnezzar to invade Jerusalem. The people of Jerusalem were treated brutally.

In North Africa, a great civilization arose that was Egypt. The historical records of ancient Egypt begin with Egypt as a unified state, which occurred sometime around 3150 BCE. The history of Egypt must include Jacob and Rachel. Jacob and Rachel have twelve sons. Leah, who first appears in Genesis 29, is Jacob's first wife and is the older sister of his second wife, Rachel. Leah is the mother of Reuben, Simeon, Levi, Judah, Issachar, and Zebulun. Rachel has two sons,

Joseph and Benjamin. Jacob's two concubines, Ziipath and Bilah, have Gad, Asher, Dan, and Naphtali. Levi and Milkah, a daughter of Aram, who was a descendant of Shem, one of the three sons of Noah, had three sons: Gershon, Kohath, and Merari. Kohath's son Amram was the father of Miriam, Aaron, and Moses. According to the Torah, the tribe from which Moses arose was named after Levi. But first, there is Rachel's son, Joseph.

The story (Genesis 37) of the important figure, Joseph, functions to tell how Israel came to be in Egypt. Joseph is good at interpreting dreams and is given a long coat of many colors as the favored son of Jacob and Rachel. His jealous brothers, with the exception of the half-brother Reuben, plot to kill Joseph. A camel caravan carrying spices and perfume is on its way to Egypt, and Joseph is sold to these merchants. The tale is complex but the end result of Joseph's ability to interpret dreams is that he rises in favor with the Pharaoh and eventually saves Egypt during a famine. Jacob's family travels to Egypt to escape a famine. Through Joseph they are allowed to settle in the Land of Goshen, an eastern part of the Nile Delta. Through the telling of the story of Joseph is how many of the descendants of Jacob, the Israelites, were enslaved or came to live in Egypt. However, the Egyptians are worse than those in Sodom and Gomorrah because they made slaves of guests.

The Israelites held to the idea that originated with Abraham and are sure that God will send as a reward if only they will behave and be faithful, a great warrior, another word for Messiah, who will come to straighten things out. Flowing under this story is a constant undercurrent wherein God will reward and protect the faithful and punish the powerful who abuse their power. Great plagues come upon Egypt. One of which is the Angel of Death who will kill all the first born. A *something*, or God, informs the Israelites to kill a lamb and take the blood and paint it all over the top of the door stop. When the Angel of Death sees this, he will *pass over* from which comes the Passover Feast.

There is a theological possibility that behind the crucifixion lies the concept that the blood of Jesus must flow as did the flow of blood of the sacrificial Israelite's lamb. The Angel of Death will be defeated.

Resurrection will happen. As a possible reference picked up by early Christianity, it is a complex story of blessings and curses, rewards and punishments, as reflected in a Promissory Covenant. The Pentateuch tells quite a story. And so do the remaining nineteen books of the Old (First) Testament!

During their captivity, the Israelites increase in numbers and became a threat to the ruling dynasty in Egypt. The Egyptian rulers ordered the killing of the firstborn of the Israelites. Amram's wife took Moses, put him in a reed basket, and placed him in a stream where he was found by one of the wives of the Egyptian ruler. She took Moses as her own and raised him in the royal household.

Moses somehow came to understand that he wasn't Egyptian but rather was related to the slaves, the Israelites. He saw an Egyptian guard mistreating the Israelites and Moses killed him. Moses, now a felon, fled along with a handful of Israelites into the desert. The escape of the Israelites from Egypt possibly occurred during the reign of Ramses II (1,304–1,237 BCE). There were many kings of the Egyptian empire named Ramses and an impressive amount of buildings, including great temples and cities.

Moses encounters a bush on Mount Horeb (Mount Sinai) in the wilderness, and it seems to never stop burning and/or be consumed by the fire. This story is told in the third chapter of the Book of Genesis. A conversation, a Pentecostal event, begins with the bush and Moses is to return to Egypt and lead more Israelites out of Egypt.

Moses is skeptical of the order given from the burning bush to return to Egypt and lead more Israelites out of slavery. He asks the voice in the bush how to convince the slaves to leave Egypt. The voice in the bush simply tells Moses to relate that his authority's name is "*I am.*" Moses returns to Egypt, and the Exodus occurs over an alleged forty years. The group he leads wanders in the desert and they increase in number. Moses came to see or understand the power of nature. Water from rocks, quail in great numbers flying in and manna as well as a great deal of grumbling from those who kept asking him why he brought them into the desert in the first place. The answer to grumbler's questions always was that which came from whatever was a *something* in the bush—the *I am who I am* (Exodus 3:14).

The end product of the conversation with a bush, Moses, and the "*something*" or God in the bush came to a handshake agreement. *I am* will be your neighbor and you will be mine. It was an Obligatory Covenant, often called the Sinai Covenant or Mosaic Covenant. There will be no penalty as in the Promissory Covenant if when *I am* brings you a blessing you don't have to give the *I am* anything in return. It would be just a couple of friends in a friendly relationship.

It was at Mount Horeb or Mount Sinai that Moses returned, with all the freed Hebrews, to receive the Ten Commandments. Most of the original group died leaving only the original leaders Moses, Joshua, and Caleb.

Moses and *I am* did agree on a *like a good neighbor* sort of thing—those Ten Commandments or the Decalogue that were a blessing, good rules to follow but rules nonetheless, significantly without the need to return God's gift in any way but also without any significantly required penalties for overlooking or violating the blessing. With no penalties, some things were just little small sins. And a whole lot easier to overlook than to always be a good neighbor. There would be no penalties but a list of *thou shall nots*. They would be ethical behaviors most likely modeled on other groups nearby such as the Hittites or the Mesopotamian laws and treaties. Moses's ancestors who date back to Jacob involved a whole lot of cousins that weren't part of those who were those Moses brought out of Egypt. The genealogical chart is rather extensive.

The *something* or God became very anthropomorphic and also became a good fix-it-man. When rain is needed, just ask. Just fix it. We are, nice but they aren't so nice, so please, dear God, just fix it. The *good neighbor* Obligatory Covenant, however, needed a re-do and became more promissorial or Abrahamic in nature. There were blessings and curses to deal with as part of the Abrahamic or Promissory Covenant. The *thou shall not* of the Decalogue would now demand a penalty.

Joshua and his army were sent off by Moses to totally destroy Jericho. He was to conquer Canaan, the Promised Land. Joshua completed the task of leading the Israelites into the Promised Land and of taking possession of it. The Israelites occupied and conquered Palestine, or Canaan, beginning in the late second millennium BCE, or perhaps earlier, and the Bible justifies such occupation by identifying Canaan with the Abrahamic promise of land and descendants as numerous as the stars. Thus Canaan is the Promised Land. The destruction of Jericho didn't work out quite as well as it might have in that Jericho is still on the contemporary maps today. The land known as Canaan today encompasses Israel, the West Bank and Gaza, Jordan, and the southern portions of Syria and Lebanon where trouble continues.

CHAPTER 7

The Rise of the Roman Empire and Jesus the Messiah

Many who migrated out of Africa and didn't remain in the Levant or Egypt areas moved West of the Sinai around 1000 BCE and eventually Remus and Romulus founded Rome as a city. The Roman Empire is generally divided into three distinct periods: The Period of Kings (625–510 BCE), Republican Rome (510–31 BCE), and Imperial Rome (31 BCE–CE 476).

The Republican Roman Empire won the three Punic Wars over a period from 264 BCE to 146 BCE which included a civilization with Greek origins, the Middle East, and included ancient Egypt establishing the large Roman Empire. The Roman Empire covered landmass from Italy, parts of Europe, the British Isles, most of North Africa and Egypt, and up into Mesopotamia and across Anatolia. It was divided into the Western and Eastern Empires by Diocletian (284–305 CE).

All the provinces of the Roman Empire were now so vast that by 285 CE, the city of Rome was no longer a feasible place to govern the empire. The Western half was governed through Milan and the Eastern half through Byzantium. Rome was a ceremonial or symbolic capital of the empire. The Eastern half flourished and the Western half eventually collapsed when it was conquered by those in Western

Europe led by the Germanic barbarian king Odoacer In 476 CE. The Eastern half remained becoming what was called the Holy Roman Empire. The Eastern half adopted Greek instead of Latin as its official language and lost much of what was the traditional character of the undivided Roman Empire. The Eastern half of the Holy Roman Empire's Emperor was Constantine (272–337 CE) who becomes a Christian (or at least supported the Christians with great privileges) and also moves his capital into this eastern region and named the capital Constantinople founded on the site of Byzantium.

The armies of Islam grow and overcome the part of the Roman Empire which had previously been ancient Egypt. Quite a few years into Christendom in 641 CE the Arab Muslim armies under early caliphs conquered Constantinople ending the eastern portion of the Roman Empire. The Arab Muslims during this time frame basically left the Christians and Jews alone. Christians were left to rule Constantinople. This particular area saw many forces come and go including the armies of the Crusades. In 1452 CE, an Ottoman sultan, a Muslim, ended Christian rule in Constantinople. Constantinople's new name becomes Istanbul in what is modern-day Turkey.

Christianity that existed at the time of Constantine can trace its roots to that recorded when Moses meets God on Mount Sinai and Muhammad on the mountain Jabal an-Nour. Intertwining of Israelite and Arab stories is the visitation of the Archangel Gabriel to both Muhammad and Mary. To Mary, the mother of Jesus and a descendant from David, some six hundred years before Muhammad, God is said to have sent the Archangel Gabriel to Nazareth with a message for Mary *and* that she would have a son, a firstborn, that she would name Jesus.

> He will be great and will be called the Son of the Most High. (Luke 1:29 NIV)

The Quran states that Jesus, the son of Mary, is a prophet sent to the Children of Israel. The Quran identifies Jesus as a Muslim Messiah, or leader and prophet, because he was sent to the people who responded to him in order to remove their impurities, the ailments of their faith, whether apparent or hidden by the permission of Allah. The most important prophets in the Islamic tradition are Jesus along with Noah, Abraham, Moses, and Muhammad. Jesus is worthy of being worshipped. Unlike Christians, Muslims see Jesus as a prophet, but not as God himself or the Son of God. Prophecy in human form for Muslims does not represent the true powers of God. Christianity takes a contrary view. Thus, like all other Islamic prophets, Jesus is one of the grand prophets who receive revelations from Allah. Sunni Muslims believe Jesus is alive in heaven and did not die in the crucifixion.

> They did not kill him, nor did they crucify him, but they thought they did, since the Messiah was made to resemble him to them. (Surah 4:1 67–158)

Jesus is crucified during the period of time in the area that was controlled by Imperial Rome (31 BCE–CE 476). The Messianic Promise seems a bit undone. History and human behavior being what it is takes what it has and makes something that makes sense of the whole matter. By the first century within the Jewish/Christian community, the view developed that the Messianic Age would witness a general resurrection of the dead, the in-gathering of all the Jews, including the Ten Lost Tribes of Israel, to the land of Israel, a final judgment and universal peace.

The ten lost tribes of the original twelve tribes of Israel may have been exiled from Israel by the Neo-Assyrian Empire about or near 722 BCE after they conquered Israel. These tribes were Reuben, Simeon, Dan, Naphtali, Gad, Asher, Issachar, Zebulun, Manasseh, and Ephraim. Only the tribes of Benjamin and Judah remained. The tribe of Levi didn't have any territory as they were considered a priestly tribe.

The Messianic Promise/Age finds expression in various *clue* words. The word Advent was adopted by the Christian community and adapted from Latin *adventus* "coming; arrival" or by translating the Greek word *parousia*. In the New (Second) Testament, this (*adventus* and or *parousia*) is the term used for the Second Coming of Christ, the Messiah. The physical nativity in Bethlehem, the reception of Christ in the heart of the believer, and the eschatological Second Coming represent three different perspectives of the coming of Christ, or the Messiah, during the season of Advent in the Christian calendar. In the strict Jewish community, such thinking and perspective are not considered as a valid start of the Messianic Age.

The question "Was Jesus the Messiah?" for Jews, Muslims, and Christians require a definition of Messiah. The vision of a Messianic Age is that, "They shall beat their swords into plowshares and their spears into pruning hooks; nation will not lift sword against nation and they will no longer study warfare" (Isaiah 2:4). A period of universal peace, in which war and hunger are eradicated, and humanity accepts God's sovereignty, is both held by Christians and Jews.

In Abrahamic religions, a Messiah is a liberator of a group of people. In Judaism, the concepts of Messianism and a Messianic Age have their origin in which a king or high priest is traditionally anointed with holy anointing oil. The majority of Christian theologies consider Jesus to be the Son of God, a concept of the Messiah fundamentally different from the Jewish and Islamic concepts. Jesus becomes considered as the Messiah, the anointed one, and in the lineage of King David. In three of the four New (Second) Testament Gospels, the only literal anointing of Jesus is conducted by a woman (Matthew 26, Mark 14, and John 12). Messiahs were not exclusively Jewish, however, and the concept of *the* Messiah as a single individual is a strictly post-biblical tradition as it is not found in the Old (First) Testament.

In Hebrew, *masiah* or *messiah* was translated into Greek as *christos* which is a title and not an indication of divinity. Christ comes from the Greek word *christos*, meaning the anointed one. In Christianity, the word *Christ* is synonymous with Jesus and is understood as meaning *the Messiah Jesus*. Jesus, the presumed Messiah, now becomes Jesus Christ, or Jesus the anointed one. *Jesus Christ* ceases to be just a title but directly connected to the concept of God, the *something*, as reflected in the Nicene Creed first adopted at the First

Council of Nicaea in June 325 CE: "And in one Lord Jesus Christ, the only begotten Son of God—being of one substance with the Father." Constantine didn't think that emperors could settle questions of doctrine that were emerging in the Christian community. He convened both the Synod of Arles and the First Council of Nicaea. If nothing else, this indicated his interest in the unity of Christianity and quite possibly indicated his claim to be Christianity's head.

CHAPTER 8

The Christian Year, Hanukkah, and Eid Al-Fitr

For Christians, the season of Advent begins the fourth Sunday before Christmas Day and is a period during which believers individually and collectively prepare for the *coming of Christ* or the Messiah. For Jews, however, since there is a continuation of wars, hunger, and without world peace, the Messianic Age as stated by Isaiah 2:4 has not begun as Christians believe it did with the birth of Jesus.

There is a general misunderstanding that the Jewish Festival of Hanukkah which often occurs about the same time as Christian Advent is incorrectly called the *Jewish Christmas*. Every year, Hanukkah or the Jewish Festival of Rededication, also called the Festival of Lights, is an eight-day celebration that falls each year on the Hebrew calendar date of 25 Kislev, which generally falls in December or late November in the Gregorian calendar. The eight-day Jewish celebration commemorates the rededication during the second-century BCE of the Second Temple in Jerusalem, where Jews known as the Maccabees had risen up against their Greek-Syrian oppressors. This revolt, the Maccabean Revolt, turned out to be a success. The Jews regained the right to practice their religion in their temples. In order to do so, Judah called on his followers to cleanse the Second Temple and light a menorah with oil that had been blessed by the high priest all night every night until the new altar could be built over the old one.

This menorah is the gold candelabrum whose seven branches represented knowledge and creation and was meant to be kept burning every night. But there was only one flask of oil left that would last for only one night. They lit it anyway, and it stayed lit for eight days, the amount of time needed to press new oil.

For Muslims, the celebration of a birth of a prophet, of which Jesus is considered one, is prohibited. Ramadan is the ninth month of the Islamic calendar during which Muslims observe a month of fasting, prayer, reflection, and community. Muslims do have a three-day celebration called Eid Al-Fitr at the end of Ramadan. It is a time to celebrate the faith, to be charitable, to visit friends and family, and to exchange gifts.

For Christians generally speaking, Advent is primarily focused on the physical nativity in Bethlehem. The physical nativity is celebrated on December 25 in modern times and is followed by a season called Christmastide that lasts for twelve days ending on or around January 6. In Western Christianity, January 6 is the feast called Epiphany. This feast commemorates principally, but not solely, the visit of the Magi (Matthew 2:1–12) and thus Jesus' physical manifestation to the Gentiles.

Epiphany season lasts forty days at the end of which the Gospel of Luke 2:22–39 relates that Mary was purified according to the religious law, followed by Jesus's presentation in the Jerusalem temple leading up to the Season of Lent. Ash Wednesday marks the beginning of Lent which is forty to forty-six days before Easter. The number forty days may be related to the forty years during which Moses leads the Israelites out of Egypt into the desert in an event called the Exodus or a period from slavery into freedom. It could also be related to the forty days of the flood in the flood narrative. 'Forty' could be just a convenient number. For Christians, it is a period when Christ is received into the hearts of believers. The beginning of Pentecost is on the fiftieth day of the Easter season. Advent, Christmas Tide, Epiphany, Ordinary Time, Lent, Easter, Ordinary Time, and

Pentecost are times during which Christians seek to accept/believe Jesus as the Messiah in their hearts.

Linguistically, a complex story as recorded in the Bible is interesting, as well. The Old (First) Testament was written in Hebrew. The Hebrew language has a feminine word *Almah*. It's the masculine word for *Elem*. The prophet Isaiah (Isaiah 7:14) could have used *Bethoula* but instead chose the word *Almah*. The word usually designated a chaste girl usually under the protection of her family, a female who just recently become fertile. Isaiah says (translated from Hebrew to English) something like "A virgin shall conceive and bear a son." The history of the writing of Isaiah is much older than the story related to the birth narratives in the New (Second) Testament. Nothing related in the New (Second) Testament was written until some thirty to one hundred or more years after the crucifixion.

The Synoptic Gospels are those that contain similar stories about the life, ministry, and death of Jesus and are Matthew, Mark, Luke) of the New (Second) Testament. They were written in Greek rather than in Latin, the prevalent language of the ruling Roman Empire. The Revelation of John, also written in Greek, does not contain any parables which is why it is not considered one of the Synoptic Gospels. It is generally accepted that none of the Synoptic Gospels with the *possible* exception of the Revelation of John whose author may have been John the Apostle were written by the original apostles. If it is accepted that the Revelation of John was written around 96 CE, then the possibility of its authorship by an original apostle comes into doubt.

Occasionally there is a *hint* of a Hebraic influence in the Synoptic Gospels written in Greek. Greece was never a civilization overcome by the Roman Empire but rather a culture of city-states. However, the language and thought patterns remained. The language of the everyday person at the time was Hebrew and/or Greek. The Jews who became Christians would be familiar with Hebrew but would use Greek as the everyday language. Paul, a Grecian Jew, wrote mostly in Greek as well as the language of the audience he was addressing. However, the non-Jews who became followers of the newly rising Jewish group called Christians would know Greek and little if any Hebrew.

Greek was translated from Hebrew then into Latin and later into the vernacular of various regions such as German or English. The *hint* of Hebraic influence, *Almah*, evolved into the English word *virgin*. At no place are the words of Jesus recorded exactly. It was all memory work or a paraphrase of what was thought Jesus said. Jesus is said to refer to his great works and never to his divinity except to a reference to being a part of the *I am*. Jesus responds to a complaint by the Pharisees. "I tell you the truth," Jesus says, "before Abraham was born, I am!" (John 8:58). There is no doubt that the Jews understood Jesus' claim to be the eternal God incarnate because they took up stones to kill Him (verse 59).

The *I am* reference might well be a reference not to "*I am God incarnate*" but rather to being a part of that created by the Creator (God) of which all things are apart. Jesus's sayings were recorded only from memory and first in Greek, then Latin, and not exactly using the same tense or exact wording, like *Almah* in Hebrew becoming *virgin* in English. Maybe the same but then maybe not *just the same*.

CHAPTER 9

The Relevance of the Christian Church as an Institution and Church as People

Clearly, much followed the first-century CE as the Christian group (Church or the people of God as opposed to *church* as an institution/building) grew in numbers, developed, and adapted. The Abrahamic-Promissory Contract which called for blessings and curses was followed, decided what became heresy and doctrine, institutionalism was strengthened and codified, contrition, and grace defined. Various views arose over time concerning these issues and many issues came to the forefront during the Reformation that occurred in the sixteenth-century CE. The Abrahamic Covenant was visited and revised emerging to look more like the Mosaic Covenant but with penalties and curses that could be overlooked and rewarded, through acts of contrition or the sacrificial aspects of the crucifixion, punishment, and absolution of sins, rewards, for all until we arrive at today.

Events that seem to encourage insularity, lack of charity, discord, and animus and thus fail Christian precepts and examples in the contemporary scene are not new. The roots, of which, reach deep into recorded history. When Jesus first reads (Luke 4:14–30) in the temple, he reads from Isaiah 61 about two persons, a male leper and an afflicted woman, both of whom were not Israelites, whom God heals. The good temple goers become upset.

Jesus's entire redemptive message that deals with good deeds and great works, the precepts, examples, good works, and teachings, starts with this temple interpretation of the Prophet Isaiah. God was interested in all of that which He created. What was perceived as *relevant* wasn't quite what the good temple goers thought. They wanted to throw Jesus out and kill him. They wished to separate themselves from such thinking. Insulation and animosity were the favored position. Unfortunately, the contemporary Christian scene reveals that the churchgoers tend to follow the example of the Temple goers and choose insularity and inhospitality rather than the acceptance of all humanity as Jesus preached using the text from Isaiah.

It might be argued, or too outlandish but possibly reasonable, that the decline or failure of Christianity today is an echo of the Flood narrative and/or the Sodom and Gomorrah stories with the failure represented by iniquity, inhospitality, adultery, pridefulness, cruelty, extortion, oppressing the poor and the needy and often, homosexuality, and not following the precepts, examples, and teachings of Jesus resulting in a decline in church attendance.

Church building doors become revolving doors and many pass through and turn around to leave through that which they arrived. For some, the church's bells ring calling the worshippers to come and worship and the worshippers refuse to go. The church's bells were told by many to be silent. They were noisy and irrelevant.

The ringing of bells calling all, whether unbelievers or believers, to worship, in such a case, was or is seen as irrelevant, or at least, perceived as irrelevant. Some might question what was believed to be true and might reasonably question what was true. Irrelevant, and possibly untrue, because a direct benefit, a value, is not seen.

A value, or perhaps called a blessing, is only an imagined phantasy. And, too, the place of worship, the church building, is perceived as *an institution* that claims that it is the only, and exclusive, place or venue that leads to a belief in or connection with God or to personal spiritual fulfillment. The *institution* becomes an impersonal entity that requires engagement and attendance. It might be perceived that a Pentecostal event where the voice of God can possibly be heard by individuals can only occur inside the *institution*. The attention is on the *institution* rather than on God/the *I am*. Individual responsibility outside the *institution/church* to worship the *I am* is seen less positively and individual responsibility/faithfulness to God and to worship God/*I am* is less important than to be devoted to the *institution*.

Ironically, it is the *institution* that is the place of learning and teaching about what the *institution* considers to be the true history and tradition of the *I am*. A disconnect occurs between the learning and the development of individual responsibility with regard to spirituality and the value of attendance. The declining attendance at places of worship seems to be increasing even among committed worship goers. Yet many, whether devoted attendees or not, still find, at root, a belief in the *I am*. And in spirituality there is the hope that the voice of God, a Pentecostal event, will be heard in their lives whether within the walls of a place of worship or not.

In contemporary Christian worshipping fellowships, the precepts, examples, and teachings of Jesus are usually mentioned; wine is turned into Jesus's blood, songs sung, sermons preached on how much God wants many to be brave, successful, and loving and saved from our bad, sinful ways. The doors of the institutional church swing wide open with those in attendance finding that the world is not so good, brave, successful, and loving. Besides, some bad things are just little sins of no great matter anyway, not to mention often a whole lot more fun to do than stop doing those bad things.

It was a great deal easier to believe in an Obligatory Covenant which only had blessings and no punishments for bad behavior than to adhere to the Promissory Covenant that contained punishments for bad behavior. No mea culpa, mea maxima culpa prayer was thought of as necessary. Senators don't act with proper behavior; kids shooting other kids at school; ransomware; migrants fleeing oppressive governments; traffic stops for no good reason at all; and disrespect for other *Homo sapiens* whose pigmentation is different. Wars and rumors of wars become front-page news.

What was relevant inside the revolving door is irrelevant, not carried and put into action and word, on the outside. The *I am* in the Mosaic Covenant, the friendly handshake of friendship and fellowship is replaced by a *something/God* to which one turns, or demands action from God, to get things fixed only to find there is a failure of response. A leaky faucet remains! The Messianic Promise is seen as illusive, irrelevant, misunderstood, not emphasized, or disregarded. It is seen as nothing important for which to hope.

For Christians, the season of Advent is a time of anticipation/beginning of the Messianic Age in a more traditional/historical sense. For Jews, it is not. Today, for many the world in general is failing and insular. Christian and non-Christian neighbors, as well as world neighbors, are limited to those in their select groups/fellowships. Those that don't look the same, don't pray the same, don't think the same, and are not welcomed. A total lack of hospitality is portrayed here, as it was in the Sodom and Gomorrah and Gibeah stories, failing Jesus's first precepts and examples when he interpreted Isaiah 61.

A parallel might also be drawn between the decline in attendance and with the Exodus story. Those who were part of the Exodus story blamed Moses for a lack of water and food. Moses calls to God saying that the people want to kill him.

What is he to do? To which God instructs Moses to take his staff (in faithfulness to God's instruction) and strike the rocks from which water flows and manna falls from the skies. A disappointing view of the Messianic Promise could very well be seen as a failure in contemporary times as evidenced by a decline of attendance at worship services.

The church/institution and beliefs proclaimed being seen as illusive, irrelevant, or disregarded because they don't address the problems of the world outside the institution of the church. But who will strike the rocks as represented by the problems of the world outside the institutional church so that peace and truth will flow? The problem facing the Exodus group was survival expressed as water and food. Contemporarily, peoples throughout the world are faced with many problems affecting survival and civility. It is the church, the people of God, who, whether churchgoers or not, must strike the problem rocks to bring forward peace and truth. There is a hope expressed in the Christian church year beginning with promises in terms of faithfulness to God/*I am* as was the case with the faithfulness of Moses in the Exodus story. And that theme is found in the meaning of Advent. The voice of God can be heard when those who can listen.

CHAPTER 10

The Past Reviewed: Looking Forward

A review of any historical past can prove to be unclear. Mythology and mysticism, a consideration of what is true and exceptional, often cloud actual historical events. The Bible and the Quran record events and are often perceived as baskets of jewels to be treasured. Who is speaking in the various texts is conditioned by the outlook of the speaker and the agenda from which the speaker speaks. A similar conditioning is exercised by the reader of those various texts. To learn from the past involves the reality that matters of human intercourse hasn't changed all that much.

History tends to repeat itself. A reliance on that presented as historical truth depends on whether the *truth* is of history's greatness or its decay. Often usurped by those who wish to project a certain viewpoint, historical facts and or events are taken hostage and modified for the viewpoint's advantage. Such must also be the case with what is written here. A people, individually or collectively, can be drawn together by referencing the past. Such gathering can result in the highest aspect of that considered as good. It can also cross a dividing line and lead to insularity and animus toward others.

A study of the past does provide a window on how people and cultures view themselves, what they valued, how they controlled themselves, and their relationships with others. The job of determining what happened in the historical past is nearly an impossible task. Many dimensions controlled and influenced the actions of peoples, cultures, and civilizations. Some of the dimensions were so subtle as to be unnoticed in the telling of a historical event. What is important to remember is that the historical past has a continuing impact and relevance on the present and the future. Therefore, the recording of the voice of God speaking to his created and the maxim of which is called the Messianic Age does shape the present and future of humanity.

God spoke to His creation as recorded in the Bible and Quran. Sometimes God spoke in dramatic fashion as in the story of Moses and the burning bush. 1 Kings 19 states that God spoke to Elijah in a whisper. There was little room for doubt that it was God. However, God doesn't always speak in such a spectacular fashion. Hearing the voice of God is often a subtle thing. Quiet moments and during the evening news might be examples of subtle encounters with the voice of God. Often it is confusing and not clear.

When is an *aha* event in conflict with present circumstances of life? Absolute positions are absolute for reason. Autocracy, dictatorships, theological maximums, ridged racial, sexual, or ethical beliefs systems are absolutely absolute as power structures. The maximum consolidation of power requires the elimination of a rival. To rely on "God said it. I believe it, and that's that" can lead to personal uncertainty and an unwillingness to see matters differently. Acts 17:24–28 states that God orchestrates His plans through the events, the decisions of life, and all the people and places. Yet God gives His created free choice. Mankind is not a puppet on a string. Predestination is a dangerous subject. Free choice is a dangerous concept if exercised without restraint. The world and all sorts and conditions of mankind contribute to confusion and uncertainty.

Throughout history there have been wars and rumors of wars.

> You will hear of wars and rumors of wars, but see to it that you are not alarmed. Such things must happen, but the end is still to come. Nation will rise against nation, and kingdom against king-

> dom. There will be famines and earthquakes in various places. All these are the beginning of birth pains. Then you will be handed over to be persecuted and put to death, and you will be hated by all nations because of me. At that time many will turn away from the faith and will betray and hate each other, and many false prophets will appear and deceive many people. Because of the increase of wickedness, the love of most will grow cold, but the one who stands firm to the end will be saved. (Matthew 24:6–13 NIV)

Animus has happened. Animus is happening. Animus seems to be a continuing thing. It is Pollyannish to think otherwise. Animus toward others will be based on differing beliefs, pigmentation, regions of origin, and religious groups burning others at the stake, divisions within various religious organizations, crusades in the name of specifically held religious beliefs, the phenomenon of a lack of charity, hospitality and acceptance, and the simple matter of taking health precautions to prevent the spreading of disease. In many quarters of the civilized world, various freedoms are held tightly. Animus toward others is often sparked based on the interpretations of those tightly held beliefs. And those tightly held beliefs can be that believed to be what is good. Absolute good or absolute evil is equally undesirable when exercised without restraint.

The freedoms mentioned in the Amendments to the Constitution such as speech, religion, press, assembly, the right to petition the government, to be secure in one's home, the right to bear arms, a speedy trial, and other guaranteed freedoms are constrained. All freedoms are not freedoms from restraint. The loss of any freedom or the absence of restraint in matters of choice can, and often does, lead to anarchy. One can swing one's fist all one wants but that freedom stops at another's nose. Freedom without restraint will and can result in the loss of initial freedom. Crusades, burning at the stake, crucifixion, the choice to live where one wants without regard to the needs and desires of others can, as examples, lead to a loss of freedom. To marry whomever one wishes, to build, to read, to proclaim a particular faith or to disavow any faith, to express one's sexuality in various ways and means are necessary freedoms but if exercised without concern for the peace, security, and comfort of others can lead to all manners of animus. Absolutes exercised without compassion and acceptance of the absolutes of others is a clear recipe for animus.

Freedom without restraint as an exercised protest and resistance of a perceived wrong will result in a continuation of wrong/violation of civility, peace, and concord among peoples. Fighting for the right and that which is good has flowing under the good and right a rushing stream of animosity and insularity. To stand in the face of being disliked, dismissed, disassociated becomes a matter of courage. The example of the life and crucifixion of Jesus may very well be a clear example of this. "Because of the increase of wickedness, the love of most will grow cold, but the one who stands firm to the end will be saved" (Matthew 24:16). To voice the right and fight the wrong of any unrestrained freedom, equality, and reconciliation among peoples will result in reconciliation overcoming animus.

The visions expressed in Jesus's reference to Isaiah 61 and that in Isaiah 2:4 are utopian in nature but values worth the fight. The Messianic Age, an age of reconciliation, is utopian in nature and a value of the great prize. Throughout the historical literature, whether Hebrew, Christian, or Muslim, divisiveness is a prominent theme. And that theme is always, or seems to be, an enemy of peace and tranquility in the human community. The desire for peace and tranquility, as a utopian belief, is called Faith. Tightly held absolute interpretations of historical perspectives as expressed in the concept of

Faith can lead to the brink of the dividing line between peace and anarchy. For many, in view of contemporary and historical events, believe the line between peace and anarchy must not be crossed. For many, this is justified with the thought that the Messianic Age has begun but is yet incomplete, is developing, is still in its beginning stage, or has yet to happen. Reconciliation between all peoples is buttressed, but not conditioned, by the appearance of Jesus, His precepts, examples, and teaching as the promise of a Messianic Age. The desire for reconciliation is the beginning of the fight for good and must be continued by all whether believers of Jesus as God is held or not.

This call to fight for the good with all one's might is supported by great energy. For some, it is the voice of God speaking, a Pentecostal event, to which one has only to listen. And listen many do without passing through the revolving doors of various religious institutions and remaining inside. The great energy is seen, accepted, or believed to be, or possibly to be, a great *something/God* which is *I am*, and I am is a part of the same. As St. Augustine put it, "We were one when we were one." We are not *I am* but a part of what is *I am*.

And regarding being "one with the one," both Jews, Christians, or Muslims, whether they are Christian, synagogue, or mosque worshippers or not, agree. The agreement is celebrated with different traditions, customs, and celebrations. Yet even these different customs and celebrations can encourage insularity and animosity rather than reconciliation and acceptance of sincerely held but differing customs and celebrations. Reconciliation is that of Jesus's interpretation of Isaiah 61. It all becomes a matter of recognizing and honoring the dividing line between peace and anarchy. All freedoms are not freedoms from restraint.

In adoration of the *I am* and to follow and proclaiming the precepts, examples, and teachings of Jesus often is seen as absurd. Human nature, it seems, tends to hold that the absurd is not doable and/or not unattainable. Atheism is the proposition that God does not exist or there are no gods. The agnostic theist believes in the existence of a God or gods but regards the basis of this proposition as unknown or inherently unknowable and becomes the basis of the rejection of the absurd.

At root, that which encompasses a desired expectation of meaning based on a belief is called *faith* whether Jewish, Christian, Muslim, or to those who do not hold to any of these traditions. In faith, what is absurdly assumed, however, may be true. To this extent, Jews, Christians, and Muslims hold to the same absurd truth that there is a Messianic Age. The vision of a Messianic Age as referenced in Isaiah 2:4 as a period of universal peace, in which war and hunger are eradicated, and humanity accepts God's sovereignty is held by Christians, Jews, and Muslim. "They shall beat their swords into plowshares and their spears into pruning hooks; nation will not lift sword against nation and they will no longer study warfare."

They differ on whether the Messianic Age has begun or is to begin. And if there is no belief in a Messianic Age, there remains a hope, a spirituality, that in life, things that matter, will get better over time. The desired expectation remains compelling, for faith is a confidence that what is expected (such as a Messianic Age) to be is, or possibly to come, will be. Faith, except for the agnostic theist who only believes what is knowable, includes hope, a spirituality, that the voice of God, a Pentecostal event, will be heard just as Jesus promised John 14:26 that the Holy Spirit would be a Helper for His people.

> But the Helper, the Holy Spirit, whom the Father will send in My name, He will teach you all things, and bring to your remembrance all that I said to you. (John 14:26 NIV)

The key word here is *helper*. God is not a fix-it man who solves all problems but will help those who help themselves.

In faith, the *I am* has a center that is everywhere and a circumference that is nowhere. If this be true, then it might be argued that is why many people don't find as necessarily relevant the institutional church or a need to worship together. Rather many, if declining attendance at church events holds true today, find relevance in spirituality and witnessing as well as serving/worshipping the Lord an individual and personal matter. The people of God, the Church, the Israelites, and the Islamic Empire of Faith need not be confined to the indoors of a church, synagogue, or mosque. The voice of God is perceived as capable of being heard at any time and in any location. Any Pentecostal event is a time to celebrate God speaking to His created individually or collectively.

CHAPTER 11

Humanity's Future

The hope during the seasons of the Christian Church year is that the Messianic Age has begun, is an actuality, or is yet to come for all. Encompassing all is the hope that the voice of God will be heard stirring the hearer to action in word and deed. St. Francis of Assisi, incorrectly, is attributed the saying "Preach the Gospel at all times. Use words if necessary." Incorrectly the saying is interpreted to say that proclaiming with words of the Gospel is secondary to following or practicing what is more important, virtuous, or faithful to the faith. Correctly interpreted is the hope to gather what is important, what is needed for the day, consider what matters much and what matters little and choose whom and what to serve and, most importantly, to preach the faith in action and words. Action and words are equally important. Social justice need not be a singular activity. Social justice is achieved by the actions of all seeking, proclaiming the good in action and words.

Surrounding the good and right is a great energy in life that struggles against animosity and insularity. It is said of the late Anglican Archbishop Emeritus Desmond Tutu of South Africa that deep in his soul he knew that good would overcome evil, justice would prevail over inequity, and that reconciliation would prevail over revenge and recrimination. Poverty, hunger, and misery can be defeated. All peoples can live together in peace, security, and comfort. All that he felt deep in his soul he fought with words and action. The armor of his words and actions was more powerful than pondering and praying for good, justice, equity, and the prevalence of reconciliation. Here lies the promise, the hope, Pollyannish that it may be, that a Messianic Age will come and will be. And come and will be can only happen when it is a value worth fighting for in word and in deed. Animus in all its forms, varieties, and permutations rather than reconciliation, is the enemy of humanity. Humanity's future depends on a Pollyannish hope! And humanity must hope!

Echoes of the phrase "Power corrupts and absolute power corrupts absolutely" ring true. Such was also the case with King David and those who surrounded him. Some of which were not of the highest caliber. Second Samuel reads in such a way that blood seems to flow from every chapter and verse. First Samuel 3 is a good example of the voice of God, a Pentecostal event, speaking to Samuel. Samuel, as an emerging prophet, is to relate God's message to Eli that the evil of Eli's sons, who were high priests along with their father, and Eli's lack of control of his sons will result in all of them not living to old age. Early death would be their punishment. Samuel is rewarded with his steadfastness to God, and the rest receive deserved punishment.

The stark reality is, if equality and reconciliation aren't prized or achieved among person-to-person relationship, within societies, between societies and nations, there will be a continuation of wars and rumors of wars. The absolute power of that which is neither good nor right will seek to destroy and dehumanize whatever courageously stands in its way. The assumption that *wars and rumors of wars* only references military action is to overlook absolute power as exercised in social, religious, business, or personal relationships. It avoids a clear picture of the evil of absolute power on any level.

Absolute power, whether on a personal, local, or national scene, often tends to present itself as the victim encouraging many to be sympathetic to absolute power's persona. On a national and international scene, such was the case in the twentieth century, Hitler in his imprisonment wrote *Mein Kampf* that notably included the Big Lie. Those sympathizers who followed Hitler overlooked the evil that was the substance of his reach for absolute power. Countless many were dehumanized socially and politically as well as reduced to ashes, to annihilation, in the ovens of Dachau. The victims did not create their victimization. The evil of absolute power created ashes of many. Many, of which, were Jews but not all were. The ashes of victims were the result of the inactivity of good failing to stand tall against the rise of evil.

> First they came for the socialists, and I did not speak out—because I was not a socialist. Then they came for the trade unionists, and I did not speak out—because I was not a trade unionist. Then they came for the Jews, and I did not speak out—because I was not a Jew. Then they came for me—and there was no one left to speak for me. (Martin Niemöller)

In the end of the tragic Nazi regime, absolute power was destroyed by fire not only what it deprecated but itself.

A common wish, a common entreaty, seen historically issued by the good is based on incorrect thinking. It involves good, rather than fighting a good fight, wanting a higher power to fight whatever evil exists. In the Christian world, the remembrance of "deliver us from evil" is carried in the brain as if it were an amulet. Similar amulets have been found throughout ancient civilizations. A reliance on "The Lord will keep you from all evil; he will keep your life. The Lord will keep your going out, and you're coming in from this time forth and forevermore" (Psalm 121:7–8 RSV) becomes a false petition or a false reliance. It becomes a trap! A trap of inactivity. To ask God to help and then do nothing in pursuit of a wish of one's own creates a scenario where nothing happens. Except it allows evil to develop as a power. Christians do believe that their God was the God who safeguards his people provided the people are involved in the struggle.

> For our struggle is not against flesh and blood, but against the rulers, against the authorities, against the powers of this dark world, and against

the spiritual forces of evil in the heavenly realms. (Ephesians 6:12 NIV)

There is a humorous tale, the source of which is totally unknown, that speaks of the essence of Ephesians 6:12 addressing the everyman's wish. Not against the powers of that which are dark or evil, but a petition for the needs of survival. The tale tells of a group of farmers who gather for prayer. They pray for rain to increase the yield of their crops. One farmer speaks to say, "Prayer is good but what we need is manure!" The tale speaks of the folly of relying only on God for increased yields. Each farmer must be involved in the process by spreading available manure on their crops. If nothing else, this tale warns against a narrow interpretation of biblical lessons. The practical and simple often must be applied.

Autocratic dictatorships rise on the backs of good when the good is disinclined to fight the good fight. Such regimes, whether in Argentina, Central America, East Asia, Europe, or arising in the United States, begin with those whose interests are centered on themselves and not on the country they wish to control. Contemporaneously, it very well might be said that the mega-disaster of the COVID crisis has created more deaths sending more to ashes, as a result of those in positions of power who had control over the situation and who, thereby, were more concerned about their own welfare than the welfare of their county's peoples. And control they have done by inciting insurrections to deflect attention from their own evil intents. Anarchist, autocratic, and dictatorial leaders often fall and fail to succeed if and when similar insurrections remove them as the evil they represent.

Anarchy, autocracy, despotism, and dictatorship can create the worst of all, the threat of global annihilation-total destruction. The nuclear option moves in two directions. One direction controls evil and the other with evil controlling good. In either direction, humanity is threatened with extinction. Although throughout history, there always seems to be a remnant who survive to carry on and seek the good. In Hope, there is reason for good to continue. To hope and then do nothing is a predicate for disaster.

Inescapable is that revealed in tracing a line from prehistory to the present. Running under that traced line is a stream of consciousness that God or gods may exist and are understood as God or gods by those living in the historical events, myths, or realities. The line also tends to confirm the maxim that history tends to repeat itself. Differences in eye shape, nose size, and hair color, family ties, clan ties, them versus us, tribe versus tribe, nation versus nation, our beliefs versus your beliefs, and brother/sister against brother/sister, all are of an incomplete list of examples confirming history repeating itself.

Church bells ring and few and fewer care; Jacob and Esau; Noah's Ark; Gibeah; Isaiah 51; Joshua 24; religion against religion; The Big Lie; good versus evil; pigmentation differences and freedoms without restraint are some examples that reconciliation is a fond realization seldom realized. The Messianic Age may be full of promises but may be too little or late for some. The desire for reconciliation expressed in St. Augustine's statement "We were one when we were one" only highlights the Pollyannish desire for unity within the human family. Wars and rumors of wars and racial, genealogical, political, and national differences as revealed throughout history ennoble a fight for the right and that which is good. The courageously ennobled fight is a fight that has flowing under the good and right a rushing stream of animosity and insularity. The inescapable reality of an absence of Hope will be a predicate for disaster. Equally inescapable is the unfortunate possibility that history is repeating itself without a Pentecostal event.

> The boy Samuel ministered before the Lord under Eli. In those days the word of the Lord was rare; there were not many visions. (1 Samuel 3:1 NIV)

No Pentecostal events in the present time are a dismal possibility. For God, if the existence of God is accepted, is the same God/Lord for all. Should the Promissory Covenant be true, there will be rewards and punishments. To stand in the face of being disliked, dismissed, and disassociated becomes a matter of courage. And in hope, courage will be rewarded in the fight against the wrong. Wrong is that which lacks civility, denies equity for all, and hates reconciliation. It takes courage to fight the good fight with both word and deed. To do otherwise is to face the fate of Sodom and Gomorrah and as a punishment be reduced to ashes, metaphorically or in reality. Here, too, a faithful remnant might remain. Lot and his family were rewarded and those less virtuous in Sodom and Gomorrah were punished, reduced to ashes. Humanity is called in hope to live every day as if it were the last for someday that can become true is neither silly nor foolish! Wrong must not triumph! If not, there be a God as is recorded in Deuteronomy 29:20, who will "blot out their names from under heaven." Humanity must hope! But even Joshua may lead to divisiveness. Yet, it may lead to reconciliation, too, and perhaps a blessing.

> But He said, "On the contrary, blessed are those who hear the word of God and observe it." (Luke 11:28 NIV)

> But if serving the Lord seems undesirable to you, then choose for yourselves this day whom you will serve, whether the gods your ancestors served beyond the Euphrates, or the gods of the Amorites, in whose land you are living. But as for me and my household, we will serve the Lord. (Joshua 24:15 NIV)

ABOUT THE AUTHOR

The years 1937 to 1959 were a time to grow—a world war, victory gardens, death of a president, a First and Second Red Scare and McCarthyism, Donald from next door dies in Korea, and 2,400 persons in a farming community had the same skin pigmentation. In 1955, a seven-foot-two-tall basketball player and a dormmate from Philadelphia had pigmentation that was not mine. A bachelor of music education was completed at the University of Kansas in 1959.

Teaching begins in 1959. JFK was assassinated on November 22, 1963; LBJ and the Voting Rights Act; the Edmund Pettus Bridge; Vietnam; MLK Jr., and Selma, Alabama were little noticed in 1965. Jonathan Daniels was murdered on August 20, 1965, who took a shotgun blast meant for a fellow civil rights worker Ruby Sales in Lowndes County, Alabama. An MS in music education was completed at the Kansas State Teachers College (Emporia) in 1966.

The years 1967–1970 made clear the virtual destruction of native cultures in Micronesia and Polynesia. Missionaries required the females to dress in neck-to-ankle dresses. Natok sings to my son of her Micronesian history and culture in tunes from the missionaries' Rodeheaver hymnbook. The mumu became a colorful, popular revolt. Japan, Cambodia, Thailand, and Taiwan were visited, where cultures remained and some were lost. The German cruiser, *Prinz Eugen*, left over from the Bikini A-bomb tests, rests on its turrets on the opposite side of the Kwajalein lagoon. Sailing on the blue Pacific over downed WWII Japanese and American aircraft was idyllic. The blood of heroes has washed away. MLK Jr. was assassinated on April 4, 1968. I carry my one-year-old son on my back for ninety days throughout Western Europe before studies began in Tennessee. A master of library science was earned in 1971 at George Peabody College for Teachers (Nashville). Arizona becomes a permanent home in 1972.

The years 1972 through 1998 were a time to make changes, not excuses in a school community where 50 percent of its students were low-income and mostly Latinx. Many students didn't have a TV or even a landline telephone. Cell phones and laptops didn't exist in the seventies. Some homes didn't have a telephone of any kind by the nineties. The best efforts were hampered by lagging technology, shortsighted leaders, sexist, racist, and elitist cultural preferences. Local, state, and federal actions, or lack thereof, created lost generations. To lose as few as possible impacted by circumstances of poverty, racism, and bigotry was a choice.

Puppies entered the scene in 1980 along with new challenges. By 1990, dog judging begins. All states, Argentina, Canada, Japan, China, Australia, and New Zealand were visited. A technological-savvy son earns a JD degree in 1992. After nearly forty years in education as a teacher, a librarian, and a university professor (included in those years a subdeacon and licensed lay preacher in the Episcopal Church), I retire in 1998 and settle in the mountains of Northern Arizona with a wife of sixty years.

Author of *Trembling Before God: Twelve Homilies Explore the Origin, Development, and Failing of Christianity Today* (Fulton Books, 2020) and *Behold, It Was Very Good* (Fulton Books, 2021).

CPSIA information can be obtained
at www.ICGtesting.com
Printed in the USA
BVHW031040140223
658482BV00005B/107